EYE'M SEW KUNFUZED

EYE'M SEW KUNFUZED

by Al Yarcho

Illustrated by
Michael Stoff

Just in Rhyme
Kettering, Ohio

ISBN 1-882203-72-0
Copyright 2001 by Al Yarcho

Additional copies of *Eye'm Sew Kunfuzed* may be ordered directly from:

Just in Rhyme
P.O. Box 20411
Dabel Station
Dayton, OH 45420

Library of Congress Control Number: 2001029227

To Jill
A splendid example of why poets write love poems

—A.Y.

To Brandon and Lindsay
You have made my life full and rich beyond my imagination...(and
I have a good imagination!) Thank you for you.

—M.S.

Table of Contents

Introduction

I have always enjoyed poetry. The rhythms and rhymes attracted my attention from the very first poem I had ever read. How poets could make words sing without music, to me, was a very special craft.

I have also always appreciated all the rhythms and rhymes that come with being a young person. All those things that come with growing up are certainly distinctive. Let's face it; there's nothing like being a kid.

With *Eye'm Sew Kunfuzed,* I have attempted to combine these two affections. Short stories and thoughts set in rhyme that young people, and even adults, can enjoy. Stories that may make you laugh, others that might make you wonder. But I tried to be sure that each entry contained the two things I believe poetry and childhood each have in common—lots of fun and a vivid imagination.

So, I invite you to come on in and have a good rhyme. Oooh—that's pretty bad, isn't it? Well, read on—it gets verse.

Eye'm Sew Kunfuzed

I can't believe my day at school, I bombed my spelling test.
I studied for it all this week and tried to do my best.
There were lots of tricky questions and it seemed notably long.
You should have seen my paper and the answers I got wrong.

The first word on the test was *sign*; I concentrated hard.
I wanted to be sure that I did not get caught off-guard.
I knew l-i-n-e spelled line and thought of nine and fine,
And answered that s-i-n-e's the way that you spell *sign*.

The next word on the list was *sue*, like when you go to court.
I then fidgeted and scratched my head; I was a worry-wart.
Then I remembered d-e-w spelled dew which rhymed with *sue*,
So on my paper I said *sue* was s-e-w.

We moved on to the next one and the word to spell was *high*.
So I remembered p-i-e spelled pie and t-i-e spelled tie.
I knew that I had this one right - on this I was home-free.
So on my paper I wrote down that *high* was h-i-e.

And then the test got really hard, my brain began to ache.
But I couldn't give up then because my spelling grade's at stake.
The next word really fooled me, there were a couple ways to go,
So I thought about it extra long and took it really slow.

The word was *foam*, it rhymes with comb - it looked funny to me
When I put it on my paper, it can't be f-o-m-b!
Then I thought of other ways to go and thought of home and dome,
Now that looked so much better, f-o-m-e must spell *foam*.

I heard what word was next to spell and really got concerned,
I know I went and blew it yes, I'm sure that I got burned.
The word was *dumb* and so I thought of words like some and come,
So I answered d-o-m-e most assuredly spelled *dumb*.

But then I thought about how come was spelled c-o-m-e,
Should h-o-m-e then spell hum, is that how it should be?
And if c-o-m-b spells-out comb, but foam's not spelled like comb,
Does that mean h-o-a-m is the way that you spell home?

The next word we were told to spell seemed easy at the time.
Our teacher looked-up from her list and said the word was *rhyme*.
So instantly I thought of how to spell lime, crime and time,
The one and only answer; r-i-m-e must spell *rhyme*.

And then she said the next word on the list to spell was *soon*,
The first thing that came to my mind were two words, June and tune.
So I answered on my paper that it's spelled s-u-n-e,
And *noon* was spelled n-u-n-e as far as I could see.

We turned in all our papers for our teacher to review,
She looked them over quickly 'til she got to you know who!
She paused for just a moment then she turned and looked my way,
And asked if I could stay a while at the end of the day.

I stayed after the day's last class, my teacher said to me,
"You made a few mistakes today, your test grade is a 'D'.
I see you tried and gave this test a lot of work and thought,
And I know you tried to give your best, but you really missed a lot."

"I can give you one more chance to take the test if you'd like to,
You can take it after school next week, one day that's good for you."
I then thanked her for the second chance, I'd take the test again,
So I studied hard all week and think all went f-i-g-n.

The Saga Of Billy Richardson

There's some strange things going on in town
This tale will shock and stun.
It all happened just a few weeks back,
To Billy Richardson!

When he told us of his story
And of his amazing find.
All his classmates thought he'd lost it,
Yes, he'd surely lost his mind!

He claimed one night as he walked home
From Jason Hartley's place,
While strolling by a baseball field
He saw lights from outer space.

He looked up toward the light he claims
And saw a large object.
It hovered over second base,
Its size he can't detect.

Then he claims another came along
And landed at home plate.
Then more and more came racing by,
They finally totaled eight.

He said they shone lights all about
But stopped when they saw him.
They focused all their beams his way,
Then the lights began to dim.

Now Billy says he can't recall
What happened after that.
He just remembers waking up
Inside a laundromat.

When we heard Billy's story
As we walked to school that day.
We were certain he'd gone crazy,
They'll come lock this boy away!

But he stuck by his strange story
While we teased him and we joked.
There were Billy stories all around,
Conversations he'd provoke.

Then strange things began to happen
No one here could quite explain.
There had to be an answer,
It was driving us insane!

It all started here in my own home,
What seemed a normal day.
But what Billy did that afternoon
Went and took our breath away!

It just happened while we watched t.v.,
That first event of note.
He changed channels from across the room
Without using a remote!

Then once in the school parking lot,
He sneezed a massive sneeze.
Six cars and two trucks started-up,
As pretty as you please!

Yet another time as we walked home
Along our normal route.
Billy let rip with a huge belch
And the traffic lights went out!

He can pick-up F.M. stations
On a filling in his tooth.
I know that it sounds crazy
But it's the honest-to-God truth!

And other times I've heard it's said,
When everything's just right.
That tooth can pick-up cordless phones
And a NASA satellite!

He's made the bells go off at school
When they're not supposed to ring.
And from all the stuff I've seen him do,
I'll believe most anything!

But through it all we've stayed good friends,
I'm adjusting to the change.
Although I must admit to you,
Things can get a little strange.

And the Billy jokes have ended,
We've realized his story's true.
So we wait with awe and wonder
To see the next thing that he'll do!

Humphrey The Hamster Is Loose

When I was in Miss Jackson's class
We had our own class pet.
A hamster we'd named Humphrey,
A pet that I'll never forget.

There's a nice big cage he lived in
And we cleaned it once a week.
We'd put him in a box those times
Which always made him squeak.

Then came a Tuesday afternoon
As we cleaned-up his place.
He jumped out from his box and then
Across the room he raced!

The class went chasing after him
But all he'd do was run.
We almost had him once or twice,
He dashed by everyone.

We all scrambled through the classroom,
We looked out into the hall.
We checked the coatroom front to back,
His name out-loud we'd call.

Then someone saw him down the hall
And 'round a corner go.
His little legs were moving fast
While we were far too slow.

We looked around all through the day
Yet never found a clue.
And when the bell rang at day's end,
We weren't sure what to do.

Next morning we all took our seats,
All quiet as could be.
We'd see the empty cage in back
And miss our friend Humphrey.

Miss Jackson tried to have us read,
We couldn't concentrate.
We'd stare at Humphrey's empty cage,
Concerned about his fate.

Then in the back of class a girl
Named Laurie asked to speak.
She said she had a wild thought,
Things just might not be so bleak.

"Miss Jackson, ma'am, if you don't mind
May I be excused from class?
I know how we can find him,
And we'll find him pretty fast!"

Miss Jackson paused then said, "Okay"
And Laurie raced outside.
And shortly she returned to class,
A dog there by her side.

At first we sat there staring,
Everyone was quite spellbound.
Then Laurie said, "We'll find him,
Because Sam's a great bloodhound!"

So Laurie took the empty cage
For Sam to get the scent.
He sniffed the air and looked around
And down the hall he went.

He sniffed along the baseboards,
He smelled under every door.
His tail was waving back and forth
As he sniffed along the floor.

Then suddenly his tail just stopped,
We'd thought he'd found our pet!
But he turned into the kitchen
To see if lunch was ready yet!

So Laurie took the empty cage
And made Sam smell again.
Back on the trail through school he went,
Sometimes back where he'd been.

Then as we turned a corner
Sammy really hit the gas!
He sprinted and turned right into
Miss Walker's English class!

A stunned Miss Walker let us in,
Confusion on her face.
We all filed in and watched Sam work
As he sniffed around the place.

He paced around the room and back,
Then to a locker door.
We thought he'd wag his tail right off!
Is this what we'd hoped for?

So Laurie opened up the door
And Humphrey there she found.
We sure were glad to see him
And that he was safe and sound.

Miss Jackson's class all clapped and cheered,
Miss Walker's class just stared.
We thanked them for their patience
And for keeping Humphrey there.

Now time's gone by since our experience,
When Humphrey ran away.
And still from time to time we'll talk
About that frantic day.

Since then we've hung a picture up
Right over by the map.
It's Sam, the class and Laurie,
Humphrey sleeping in her lap.

I've Been Around
The World And Back

22

I've been around the world and back,
I've seen all there's to see.
I've seen our planet's future,
I've been part of history.

I was there when God created Earth,
I know our galaxy.
I roamed the Earth with dinosaurs
And rode with Cherokee.

I was there when Lincoln freed the slaves,
I know Thomas Edison.
And I went across the Delaware
With General Washington.

I have explored the polar ice caps.
Traveled down the Amazon.
Safaried in the jungle,
Seen the beach along San Juan.

I was with Wilbur and Orville
When their plane got off the ground.
And I was on the lunar surface
When Neil Armstrong came around.

I was there for World Wars I and II,
And the war between the states.
I saw the fighting in Korea
And the deserts of Kuwait.

I've seen Babe Ruth hit a homer
And seen Michael Jordan jam.
In fact I've seen most every sport
From here to Amsterdam.

I've seen how they make movies,
I know how to make grape gum.
I know how earthquakes come about
And where table salt comes from.

I can perform a little magic,
I know how to make guitars.
I can tell you average temperatures
Of Jupiter and Mars.

I have seen a lot of places,
I have met history's best.
The world is at my fingertips,
Everything can be accessed.

For a kid that's only twelve years old
You might think that's pretty hard.
But it's really very easy,
I just use my library card!

The Christmas Program

Of all the friends I've ever had there's one I'd never trade.
Amanda is my true best friend, she has been since first grade.
We have so much in common and together we have fun,
So when folks ask who's my best friend I tell them she's the one.

Together we'd been practicing for our school's Christmas show.
We're singing in the choir and to rehearsals we would go.
The show was only days away, there still was lots to do.
We're singing many Christmas songs; the band's performing, too.

The songs that we were singing were the ones that you all know,
There's *Oh Little Town of Bethlehem, Greensleeves* and *Let It Snow.*
We're also singing *Silent Night* and more than I could tell,
But Amanda's favorite that we sang; the song *The First Noel.*

She said she always liked that song, its words and melody.
And she really liked the way our teacher changed the end to be.
We sang the chorus twice after the end of the last verse
And Amanda always sang it to the whole wide universe.

We practiced a while longer 'til the band needed to play,
And we stepped off from the risers and about to go our way.
Then I saw Amanda lying on the stage; tears 'bout to flow,
"I slipped and fell, my foot sure hurts, I move it - it won't go!"

We called for help and people came to see what they could do.
They put an ice bag on her foot that instantly turned blue.
Then her mother came and took her to a hospital nearby,
I could see her as they drove off trying real hard not to cry.

We got a call at home that night from Amanda's mom and dad.
They said Amanda sprained her foot; she'd sprained it really bad.
She'd have to stay at home they said, to school she could not go.
But she planned to make it back in time for our big Christmas show.

I volunteered to take work to Amanda's every day.
We'd talk about our class and all she missed while she's away.
And as the week went on she felt her foot was healing well,
She'd be on stage that evening, she's ready, she could tell.

The big night came and everyone was pleased the place was packed.
The band was set-up to the left, the risers all were stacked.
We lined-up in the hallway to walk out and take our place,
Amanda led on crutches, foot wrapped tightly in a brace.

The evening was just perfect and our singing was first rate.
Each song sounded outstanding, everything was going great!
Then it struck me like a ton of bricks, I'm sure my face turned white.
I forgot to tell Amanda there was a change made for the night.

The change was in *The First Noel*, she won't know what to do.
We weren't singing the chorus twice as she had been used to.
We'd reach the end, she wouldn't stop, she'd just keep right on going.
My throat went dry and I'm quite sure my nervousness was showing.

When we finished the first chorus I then glanced Amanda's way.
I felt so helpless standing there but there I had to stay.
And sure enough, she sang on, her voice first soft and low.
I saw her face turn crimson red, from there where would she go?

She looked around the choir with a stunned look on her face,
But she never stopped her singing and she never lost her place.
She realized she'd gone too far, the damage had been done,
So she belted out that chorus like she'd practiced since day one.

Her voice carried throughout the hall, each note in perfect tone.
The audience sat silent while she finished all alone.
Then when the song was over the whole crowd stood up and cheered,
Thank goodness things did not turn out the way that I had feared.

When I caught-up with Amanda behind stage after the show,
I told her I was very proud, more than she'd ever know.
She stood there looking mad at first, then told me with a grin,
"I hope you liked my solo 'cause I won't try that again!"

But the next year at the Christmas show we got to sing once more.
And Amanda sang *The First Noel* just like she did before.
Since then for Christmas, at our school, we're very proud to say,
They sing *The First Noel* the way Amanda did that day.

If I Were President

I've thought a lot about this and
It is my full intent.
To get myself elected our
Nation's next president.

I think the things that I'd change
Would get me everyone's vote.
They'd run to cast their ballot
From Fort Worth to Terre Haute!

'Cause when I'm in the White House
Some new rules would then apply.
I'll list them here in order,
Allow me to clarify.

Spinach, beets and okra
Would no longer be in stores.
And stewed tomatoes wouldn't
Be permitted anymore.

School would last one hour,
It would start each day at noon.
And I'd make an extra Christmas
In the early part of June.

Drinking fountains everywhere
Would only serve root beer.
I'd make a law that summer lasts
For tens months of the year.

PRESIDENT

Homework would no longer be,
There'd be no set bedtime.
Cheeseburgers and ice cream cones
Would only cost a dime.

You'd get your driver's license
On the day you turn thirteen,
And my older sister gets the job
Of keeping my room clean.

There would be Sunday comics
In the paper every day.
And to get into the movies
Thirty cents you'd have to pay.

I hope you'll vote me president,
I'll be the best we've had.
And I'll start my campaign shortly,
If it's okay with Mom and Dad.

The Baseball Game

I'm from a town in Florida, its name is Lanagan.
And although I don't reside there now, it's where my life began.
I haven't been there for a while, I live so far away,
But I hope I get the chance to go and visit home someday.

I often talk to relatives and friends that still live there.
They keep me up to date on things and all the news they share.
But it surprises me that to this day back in my old hometown,
A baseball game I played in once was still the talk around.

I was just a Little Leaguer and our team was pretty good.
As we headed for the playoffs things looked great from where we stood.
For the first big game our rival was a team from Tampa Bay,
It was sure to be exciting and I couldn't wait to play.

The big day came, we took the field, the stands were all sold out.
And as the teams were introduced the crowd would scream and shout.
Then as the game got underway we saw that this would be,
A match that would be very close; a thrilling one to see.

We battled back and forth and back, the game was nip and tuck.
The teams were playing hard but in a scoreless tie were stuck.
My team came up to take our bats in the top of the fifth inning,
We realized that one lone run could help our chance of winning.

Nick McGee had led things off with a hit to centerfield.
Then their pitcher lost control and a base on balls he'd yield.
So there we had two men on base and Josh Hayes up to bat.
Josh was our best hitter; we would score in nothing flat!

The Tampa pitcher threw toward home while Josh was getting set.
We heard the sound of a sure hit when ball and bat were met.
But their man at third made one great play and touched the bag, one out,
Then threw a fastball toward first base, the outcome was in doubt.

The ump said Josh was safe at first, it sure was a close play.
But the manager of Tampa's team did not see things that way.
He ran out on the field and to the umpire he screamed,
Our man was out, by a full step, his call was blaspheme!

Then the other coaches from their team joined in the argument.
They yelled and screamed and told the ump about their discontent.
But then the parents of both teams joined in the shouting fray,
Trying to out-yell the rest so they could have their say.

We players stood out on the field, all we could do was stare.
People running back and forth and some would even swear!
Then the umpire had heard enough, removed his mask and sighed,
He said this game was over; yes, both teams disqualified.

If you think the coaches yelled before, you should have heard them then!
And the parents added to the clash and bellowed once again.
They followed the umpire as he tried to leave the scene,
Coaches, parents shouting as they tried to intervene.

Well, we were left out on the field not knowing what to do.
Should we join the squabble or just wait 'til they were through?
We looked across to Tampa's team and they looked just as puzzled,
No one said a word as if our mouths had all been muzzled.

Then someone on the other team said, "Why don't we just play?"
"They'll be arguing forever, this could last the whole darned day!"
So we took the field and started back just where the game had ended.
To us it didn't matter that our teams had been suspended.

We played the game, it still was close, we never paid attention,
If the fueding still went on or was it over and done?
And as we reached the eighth inning the parents all came back,
Amazed that we were playing and the game was still on track.

They stood there and they watched us, no one said a single word.
The sound of playing baseball was the only sound you heard.
And they waited 'til we finished, no one tried to stop us play.
Why couldn't they behave like that a little earlier that day?

We finished up and Tampa won, the score was four to three.
We shook their hands after the game; the way it ought to be.
And the legend of that afternoon went down in baseball fame,
Two teams who didn't care who won, they just loved to play the game.

The Year I Got Sick
For Halloween

My friends and I were walking home
From school one cool fall day.
It was George and Jimmy, Steve and I
And we talked along the way.

We're thrilled that in just two short days
Halloween was finally here.
We couldn't wait to trick or treat,
We'd waited one whole year.

Jimmy said he's looking forward to
Dressing-up just like a pirate.
Steve said he'd be an astronaut
And George just wasn't sure yet.

The next day while we were in school,
We still were counting down,
The hours until trick or treat -
We'd sure cover lots of ground.

But as the day went on at school
I started feeling queasy.
My head felt hot and my ears rang
And my stomach was uneasy.

Mom picked me up and home we went
Where I went straight to bed.
I hoped a nap would helps things out
And ease my aching head.

But at the end of that long day
I went from bad to worse.
I wished a way existed to
Make days go in reverse!

When I awoke the next day
I still wasn't "in the pink".
I can't believe that I got sick
On Halloween, that stinks!

When evening came and darkness fell
The beggars all came out.
I heard them laughing in the street,
All having fun, no doubt.

And from my place there on our couch
I'd see the beggars come.
Their bags all filled with candy bars,
Popcorn balls and gum.

And then a pirate rang our bell
As he gave his bag a heave.
I could see that it was Jimmy,
Only where were George and Steve?

"Hey Jimmy, where's the other guys?"
I asked him from my seat.
But all he said was, "Have to go,"
And sped out toward the street.

Then shortly after Jimmy left
And more kids came around,
Steve and George came knocking
Saying Jim could not be found.

I told them he had just been by,
He didn't stay a minute.
So whatever Jim was up to here,
We sure didn't get it!

Then Steve and George said, "Get well soon"
And raced into the night.
A few more kids came later,
How I wished I'd felt all right.

But long after the begging ceased
Our doorbell chimed once more.
I peered out through the window
And saw Jimmy at the door.

"Why aren't you with your candy?"
I asked Jim as he stepped in.
He dragged a bag inside telling
Me everywhere he'd been.

"I must have seen a million homes,
You should have seen me run!
I'd love to know how far I went
Now that all's said and done."

"But I told each house about your luck
And asked them if they could,
Put in an extra treat for you
And most folks said they would."

Then I ran home and split the loot,
So here's your share, my friend.
You can have it when you're better,
But you have to wait 'til then!"

I tried to find a way to thank him
For his generosity.
Then he just said, "Hey, we're best friends,
You'd do the same for me."

Buford and Jade

I have a tale to tell you that I'm sure you'll think's not true,
But it happened in my own back yard, my neighbors saw it too.
It started when our dog had pups, there's six when all were told,
Then the cat next door had kittens when those pups turned three days old.

The puppies and the kittens soon grew big enough to walk.
They kept us really busy, seems we chased them 'round the clock.
As they started to explore their homes and play in their back yards,
Keeping track of each of them was getting pretty hard.

Then a cute pup we'd named Buford and a kitten they'd named Jade,
Went too far while playing and to the other's yard they strayed.
Buford joined the kittens and so Jade took Buford's place,
Neither of them noticed they were in the other's space.

We discovered what had happened when we called, "Buford, come home,"
He just went back to Jade's place and then Jade back here would roam.
They'd decided they were happy where they were and that was that,
Jade was happy with the pups and Buford with the cats.

As they grew you sure could see how each was quite confused.
It sure was fun to watch them and they kept us all amused.
But when your dog likes cat food and he plays with rubber mice,
You know you have a problem, except here we had it twice!

Jade will sit under a tree and chew on a big bone.
She'll chase cars driving down the street as if that street's her own.
Buford chases birds around and bathes just like a cat,
What do you think that you would do with pets that act like that?

Now Jade and Buford each have grown still thinking they're the other,
And we're curious if other pets would think they're one another.
So we think we'll try a new switch and we bet this will be neat,
We're swapping a young guinea pig with a brand new parakeet.

A Word A Day

This all started with my sister,
Yes sir, she's the one to blame.
We'd been playing lots of Scrabble®
And she'd beat me every game.

So I decided I'd take action,
I'd no longer hear her boast.
The next time that we add the score,
We'd just see who has the most!

My strategy was simple,
I decided that the way,
To finally beat her fairly
Was to learn a word a day.

But I wouldn't learn just any words,
I'd go for those bizarre!
I could see her going crazy
'Cause she won't know what they are.

So I took our dictionary
To my room and left it there.
I'd look up words I thought would work,
Before I said my prayers.

I must admit I was amazed
At the variety of words.
There were words that looked like gibberish
And others looked absurd.

I noted all the words I liked
That were easier to spell.
I knew that when we'd play next time,
I'd beat her - I could tell.

I didn't have to wait too long,
One dreary, boring Sunday,
She brought the game into the room
And asked me if I would play.

I said I didn't want to play,
Perhaps later, not just now.
I didn't want to seem too eager,
But she kept asking anyhow.

Well I finally said I'd play her,
I sure made it seem a chore.
But it helped me think of all the words
I'd learned the week before.

She prepared the board for playing,
She was very confident.
I'm sure she planned to cause me
Aggravation and torment.

I started-off with no odd words,
I played just like before.
Then waited 'til the time was right,
'Twas sure worth waiting for!

And when that time was perfect,
I began my battle with,
A strange word I discovered,
With my tiles I spelled-out *kith*.

Well, my sister thought I'd cheated
So she went to look it up.
When I asked her if she'd found it
All she mumbled back was, "Yup."

That sure really had her rattled,
She was quite stunned, frozen stiff.
And then I stupified her with
My next word, I put *skiff.*

Then she really blew a gasket
When I spelled the word *ecru,*
Then *haft,* then *stile,* then *tocsin,*
She was sure those words weren't true!

You could see she wasn't happy,
This wasn't going as she'd planned.
And I thought she just might hit me
When I spelled-out *ampersand.*

I then followed-up those answers
With *abaft, sanctum* and *kerf.*
She got so mad that she turned blue,
She looked like Mama Smurf!

Then after I used *rebus* and
Bolus, hoyden and *yew,*
She told me that she'd had enough,
I won - the game was through!

You can imagine how I felt then,
What a splendid victory!
And I asked her when she thought our next
Big Scrabble® game would be?

She told me it would be a while
'Til she'd do that again.
She would tell me when she's ready,
So I'd have to wait 'til then.

It's been weeks since my big triumph
And we haven't played one game.
But the dictionary stays nearby,
I'm still reading just the same.

Because I have to tell you,
Learning words can sure be fun.
It can help you with your school work
And it impresses everyone.

But there's another time it's handy,
Yes sir, this I must admit.
You can call someone a *golem,*
And I'd bet they won't get it!

I Have A Really Good Feeling
I'm In Awfully Bad Trouble

I've really gone and done it now,
I've messed things up real well.
I'm sure my folks are mad at me,
Although it's hard to tell.

They haven't had much time to yell,
Our house has been a zoo.
Three t.v. stations have been here,
The paper's been here, too.

They're coming here because of me
And what I've gone and done.
Let me tell you the big mess I'm in,
The grounding's just begun.

And although I shouldn't say this now
'Cause mud is my new name.
But I don't think that I should go
And shoulder all the blame.

Because I'm made to share a room
With my big brother Wayne.
He's always pushing me around,
Sometimes he's one big pain.

Then I had this great idea
That would separate our space.
He could stay there on his own side,
And I'd have my own place.

So I worked real hard all summer
Mowing lawns and washing cars.
And I saved up all my money,
I filled-up six jelly jars.

Then with the money I went out
To yard sales far and near.
Garage sales and flea markets
Were my pastime all that year.

I purchased every box I found
Of Lincoln Logs®, each one.
And I didn't stop until I had
Enough to get things done.

So I waited until Wayne was gone,
To Boy Scout camp he went.
Then I worked hard both day and night,
Not one minute was misspent.

I took those logs and built a wall
That split our room in two.
Then took some old Erector Sets® and
Made a door I could pass through.

I used some more Erector Set®
To build a window that would work.
Then I could close it anytime
He was acting like a jerk.

I sure was proud of my new room,
My parents never knew.
That is until the job was done
And my brother's trip was through.

When he came home and told our folks
What I had done upstairs.
They stormed up to our bedroom,
I stayed behind and said a prayer.

I was in a lot of trouble
Until word had spread around.
That's when the t.v. people came,
I was the hottest news in town.

I was featured on the evening news,
The paper had me on page one.
They said they'd never seen a case
Where this was ever done.

But my parents don't know everything,
There's more to what they see.
I don't know how to tell them
Or when the best time's gonna be.

'Cause when they hear what else I've done
Who knows what they will do?
See, they don't know when I built this
I used a case of super glue.

Are We There Yet?

(Sung to the tune of *Are You Sleeping?*)

Are we there yet?
Are we there yet?
I'm so bored,
In this Ford.
How much farther is it?
We've done nothing but sit,
All day long.
All day long.

Are we there yet?
Are we there yet?
How much more?
I'm so sore.
We've been driving all day,
Did you go the wrong way?
Are you sure?
Are you sure?

Are we there yet?
Are we there yet?
If I may,
May I say?
Gotta find a bathroom,
'Fore my bladder goes boom.
Hurry please.
Hurry please.

Are we there yet?
Are we there yet?
Back at noon.
You said soon.
Aren't you getting tired?
We're sure getting wired.
Let us out!
Let us out!

Are we there yet?
Are we there yet?
I'm car sick.
Let's stop quick.
Feeling like I could die,
Next time could we please fly?
Or stay home.
Let's stay home.

Today I'm Going To Do It

(For Jimmy)

Today I'm going to do it,
Yes, I know there's a lot to it.
I tried twice before and blew it,
But today I'm going to do it.

Today I'm going to nail it.
There's no way you'll see me fail it.
And you won't see me high-tail it,
'Cause today I'm going to nail it.

I know that I can do it.
I've planned and thought all through it.
There's no way to misconstrue it
Sir, today's the day I do it.

On this day I'll make it.
Yes, I know it's work - can't fake it.
And so please don't go mistake it
That today's the day I make it.

Today I'm going to do it.
I'm about to try and true it.
I'll give it the ol' one-two it.
I can't wait until I do it.

I'm ready, yes I'll stick it.
I'll slam dunk and then drop-kick it.
I'm all set to go and sic it,
'Cause today's the day I stick it.

I know I can achieve it.
I'll make it - I believe it.
Anyway that you conceive it
Friend, today I will achieve it.

Today I'm going to do it.
Yes, I know there's a lot to it.
I tried twice before and blew it,
But today I'm going to do it.

Today's the day I made it.
I hung in there and stayed it.
What a feeling - wouldn't trade it!
'Cause today's the day I made it.

Al Yarcho has been involved in marketing and advertising throughout most of his professional career. He has written numerous local radio and television commercials, some featuring his imaginative poems. An affection for both young people and poetry inspired Yarcho to assemble *Eye'm Sew Kunfuzed,* his first collection of poems written especially for children. Al and his wife, Jill have three children and a granddaughter. They reside in Kettering, Ohio.

Michael Stoff has been in full-service advertising/design for over twenty-five years. He has won numerous local regional and national awards under his own banner of Michael Stoff/Creative and is a past president of the Dayton (Ohio) Advertising Club. Michael resides in Dayton with his two children, Brandon and Lindsay.